THE SIN SYSTEM OF OUR WORLD

The Basic Gospel As Seen Through The Eyes of A Native New Yorker

BY - ED STEELE

Copyright © 2008 by Ed Steele

The Sin System Of Our World
The Basic Gospel As Seen Through The Eyes
of A Native New Yorker
by Ed Steele

Printed in the United States of America

ISBN 978-1-60647-343-6

All rights reserved solely by the author. The author guarantees all contents are original and do not infringe upon the legal rights of any other person or work. No part of this book may be reproduced in any form without the permission of the author. The views expressed in this book are not necessarily those of the publisher.

Unless otherwise indicated, Bible quotations are taken from the Revised Standard Version (RSV) of the Holy Bible. Copyright © 1972 by The American Bible Society, New York.

www.xulonpress.com

Introduction

According to the "American Heritage Dictionary", the word <u>sin</u> is defined in the following way: "1) A transgression of a religious or moral law, especially when deliberate; 2) Any offense, violation, fault or error."

What I will attempt to do in this writing is to show that sin is more than just what is described in the dictionary, that is, sin is more than just the violation or disobedience, as it were, of some religious laws. Sin is a life-style; sin is a part of us, it is a part of our character; it is a world system in which we all live, work, and play each and every day. Ultimately, sin is the reason for which we all need Jesus Christ.

It is my hope that this message will be clear enough and in plain English so that everyone can have an understanding of what our condition as sinners is all about. I do not get into any heavy theological discussions since I am not a theologian. I do not try to persuade people to attend one particular church or denomination over another. Some of the things I address in this work are clearly of my own opinion, but like the Apostle Paul, I believe I have the Holy Spirit in the expression of my views.

I hope you find the basic gospel message enlightening in a way that you may never have thought of before.

Contents

Introduction v

Contents vii

I   Jesus Saves 9

II How We Sin 13

III The Sin System 29

IV The Sin System (cont'd.) 37

V Sex, Love & Marriage 49

VI What Is The End Of It All? 67

Bibliography 81

Epilogue 83

I

Jesus Saves

Way back in the 1960's, the decade that I consider to be the most exciting of all time and probably will never be duplicated, there sprung up amongst members of the hippie community a religious fervor called "The Jesus Movement". The people in this movement were not your ordinary Sunday church-going types who always wore a shirt and tie and believed in keeping everything in status-quo. Simply speaking, they were hippies with their long hair and blue-jeans who somehow had come to have a religious awakening that "Jesus is just all right" as the Doobie Brothers once sang.

Among the many things that the Jesus movement did was to go around evangelizing and telling everyone that "Jesus Saves". As a young person in my early teens at the time growing up in New York City, whenever I saw someone wearing that big red button which proclaimed "Jesus Saves", I thought to myself, "he or she must be one of those Jesus freaks." Of course I didn't bother to actually think about what the content of the message that "Jesus Saves" meant for me. This wouldn't happen for me until a little later in life when I was in college.

But here is the bottom-line question that everyone needs to have an answer to: what does it mean that "Jesus Saves"? Does He save money in a bank? Does He save food stamps? Does He save discount coupons? Of course the answer to these questions is no; this is not what we're talking about.

When we say "Jesus Saves", we're saying that He saves you from yourself. Now you might ask, what does that mean? It means everything that the Bible tells us about our condition as sinners. Paul says "All have sinned and fall short of the glory of God." (Romans 3:23) Solomon says in Ecclesiastes "Surely there is not a righteous man on earth who does good and never sins." (Ecclesiastes 7:20)

In essence, we miss the mark; we are unable in all of our human strength, whether physically or mentally, to try to be as good as we can be in order to live up to God's standards for us. Thus, Jesus saves us from our condition - utter hopeless sin that never ceases to exist in one form or another. As we shall see, and as I stated in the introduction, sin is more than just our violation of a certain set of rules and regulations. Sin is a world system; it is a way of life; it is the very fabric of our being; it is who we are - and without Christ, we are all lost.

A Gospel Review

So yes, Jesus saves. He did this by His sacrificial death on the cross. Without this act, we would all be condemned to eternal death. This act of a sacrifice for sins is first spoken about in the Old Testament in the book of Leviticus, chapter 16. The ancient Israelites, God's chosen people (Deuteronomy 7:6-8), show us the way. Here in Leviticus, we see the use of two goats. One is killed as a sacrifice, the other goat is cast into the wilderness with the sins of the people placed on it by the laying on of the hands of the priest Aaron. This was a prototype of what Jesus was to do for us. He shed His blood for us as an atonement for our sins (Hebrews 9:22), and He was cast into hell with the sins of the whole world upon His head. For a temporary moment in time, He was separated from His Father in heaven (Mark 15:34).

His death was a substitute for us. Putting it in criminological terms, it was as if all of us were condemned to die a capital punishment whether by lethal injection, the electric chair, hanging, or whatever for the crimes we committed. Then this guy Jesus comes along and says "wait, don't push the button yet - this guy's been granted a pardon by the governor; but more than that, I'm going to take his place and pay for the crimes he's committed." What a break! What a reprieve! What a redemption!

As a side note, Jesus' sacrifice was a perfect one because Jesus was perfect. He was tempted in every way like ourselves but did not give into the temptation. He did not come to abolish the law, but rather to fulfill the law. (Matthew 5:17) He was and is divine - the second person of the blessed trinity, true God and true man - an unexplainable mystery. If it were not so, if He wasn't divine, then His sacrifice would not have been a perfect one. He would not have been the sacrificial lamb without spot or blemish. We then would all still be in our condemned state of sin and without hope. All Jehovah Witnesses, all Mormons, all members of "The Way", groups which don't recognize Jesus' divinity, should take note of this.

Is There Any Good In Us?

When I was a student in Hunter College in New York during the 1970's, I took a course one semester called "Transactional Analysis", or "TA" for short. The basic tenet of TA is that everyone is naturally good natured (the "I'm Ok - You're Ok" theory), but that our interaction with one another becomes askew when we come from the wrong reaction. According to the TA theory, this happens usually because of something going on inside of us or due to something that happened to us, perhaps from someone else, which thus causes us to interact in a negative way with one another. I'm over-simplifying it here, but for the purposes of our discussion, let me say that just as with other psychological theories, there are elements of truth in TA. TA gives a model of how one can interact with another - "the Parent, Adult and Child model". The goal is that everyone should learn to interact with one another from their "adult" side which generally is the more mature way, whereas the "child" and the "parent" sides of our personalities cause us to interact in less positive ways in different degrees.

The thing that TA doesn't address is the aspect of sin. As far as TA is concerned, every negative action or reaction is blamed on something else. Man is basically good; according to TA it's just that somebody came along and messed us up in our lives because of something that that somebody was going through in their own life. Well that something, according to scripture, is called sin. It's man's imperfection, it's man's selfishness - always desiring to get something for himself no matter what the cost, no matter who it hurts. Ultimately, it's man's subconscious desire to be his own god and do whatever he wants to do. The Bible calls this pride. We're too prideful to bow down to the true and living God, the creator of the universe, and to follow His way for living.

Obviously, there *is* some good in man. We see goodness expressed everyday in various charities. We see how people, non-religious people, contribute to good and noble causes each and every day. We see how various professions, the medical and teaching professions just to name two, contribute to enhancing life in positive ways. So yes, there is some good in man.

Even the Bible expresses this. Paul says in Romans 2:14-16 "When the gentiles who have not the law do by nature what the law requires, they are a law to themselves, even though they do not have the law. They show that what the law requires is written on their hearts, while their conscience also bears witness and their conflicting thoughts accuse or perhaps excuse them on that day when, according to my gospel, God judges the secrets of men by Christ Jesus." (RSV)

And yet, despite the fact that we see goodness in man, expressed daily in various ways as just mentioned above, we still have to deal with the element of sin in our lives. The scriptures point to our imperfections and show us that all of our good deeds could never measure up to what God truly desires for us. (Isaiah 64:6)

In the next chapter, I will begin to examine some specific aspects of this thing called sin and how it is manifested in us. As you read on, however, I would say to you to not get discouraged, particularly if you have an awakening and start to see yourself in all that I'm talking about. We are all in the same boat. The answer to our dilemma is closer than you may never have imagined before.

II

How We Sin

One of the first ways we are able to recognize our true human condition as imperfect beings is when we look at the "Ten Commandments". We know how we received the ten commandments; the book of Exodus chapter 20 gives us the account of how Moses ascended to the top of Mount Sinai during the time of the ancient Israelites wandering in the desert after their flight from Pharaoh's Egypt. It was in this desert experience that God laid down the law to His people on how they should live. As the story of the ancient Israelites continues on in the Old Testament, one thing becomes evident. The people, God's people, were unable to perfectly keep the law. Time and again they failed in one area or another. Even before Moses came back down from Mt. Sinai with everything that God had given him, the people were already worshipping false gods and images made of gold; all this despite everything they had seen and experienced God do for them up until this time, the crossing of the Red Sea being just one of those experiences.

The story of the ancient Israelites is a mirror to ourselves today. How have we violated God's laws despite the many blessings He has bestowed on us throughout time? Let us now look a little deeper into this maze of sin.

Amongst all the literature I read as a young Christian while in college, one piece of work that helped me on my way to gaining a more clear understanding of what the Christian walk is all about was a book entitled "Basic Christianity" by John Stott. One part of his book gives some interesting insights into the ten commandments and how they relate to us in our current world. I will attempt to paraphrase here in this chapter on some of John Stott's insights. So let us now look at the commandments themselves.

#1 "I am the Lord your God…..you shall have no other gods before me."

Do any of us consciously worship strange or pagan gods today? Maybe not. But here's how we violate this law. Every time we deliberately break one of God's laws, we play god to ourselves. It's like we're saying to God that we don't agree with His standards, so we make our own standards. In essence, we make ourselves god. The real God no longer has first place in our lives'. We do what we want, thus putting ourselves in the role of god. Anything that takes first place in our lives besides God has the potential for becoming our god. It could be our careers or jobs; it could be a relationship; again, anything that replaces our relationship with the true God of heaven and earth as our first priority in life, this becomes a god to us. Indeed, a good example of this is money. Has the desire for more money become a god in your life?

#2 "You shall not make for yourself a graven image."

The background of this commandment has to do with God trying to prevent His children Israel from doing what their captors the Egyptians had done, and that was the making of golden images of animals and even of Pharaoh himself for the purposes of worshipping them. God is more than what is portrayed in any image or statue. He certainly isn't any animal, which unfortunately is still portrayed even today in image form in some eastern religions.

The Roman Catholic Church, the church of my youth, still has many statutes of saints and even of Jesus in most of its buildings. How many times have any of us seen people praying before these statutes as if the very being of those saints were present in those images. This is exactly what God was trying to prevent. The Bible says that God is a spirit, and those who worship Him will worship in spirit and in truth. (John 4:24) God is bigger than any statute. God doesn't want us to put our image of Him in any box. This is the essence of this commandment.

Think about this for a moment: was Jesus white with blonde hair and blue eyes? Was He olive-skin, you know, like some good looking Italian guy? Was He black? Well guess what. No where in the Bible is a human physical description given of how Jesus looked while He was here on earth. Why do you think this is? The answer is simple. Our relationship with Him wasn't to be based on the way He looked. Our relationship is supposed to be a heart relationship, having nothing to do with physical appearance. It's ok to have artistic renditions of figures of biblical history, but that's all they're supposed to be - an artistic rendition, not objects of worship in and of themselves.

#3 "You shall not take the name of the Lord your God in vain."

The obvious violation of this commandment is how we curse and use God's name with foul words. But here again, it's more than that. Just as with the 1st commandment, we violate the spirit of the law whenever we sin in any area. If we call ourselves Christians, that is, if we are true believers in Jesus, believers in who He is and in what He did for us, then we shame His name, if you will, whenever we sin. The Bible calls us ambassadors of Christ. An ambassador is suppose to represent what their country stands for. Do we represent Christ in a proper way when we sin? On the contrary, we take His name and shame it.

#4 "Remember the Sabbath day by keeping it holy." (NIV)

Of all the commandments, this one has obviously been disregarded the most in our current world. For the Christian church, Sunday is still considered to be the day of worship. Of course for the Jew, especially the Orthodox Jew, Saturday is their Sabbath. But as we look at our world, especially in certain urban areas, we see that the Sabbath day has almost become like any other day of the week.

Retail businesses continue to do business; public services, some of which are obviously needed, continue to work. Even trading on Wall St. continues though not to the extent as on a weekday. Broadway shows do some of their biggest business on weekends. And of course, the world of sports is big on weekends. The point is, the Sabbath no longer is truly the Sabbath.

In a spiritual sense, this commandment has caused some controversy. As Christians, we know that we are under grace and not the law, and that really any day of the week could be our day of worship, not just Sunday. But again, the question is are we really taking that time out from our busy world, no matter what day of the week it is, to worship and focus on the Lord. Some smaller areas of our country such as in rural areas may be the only ones left who totally shut down for the Sabbath.

Ultimately, I believe as individuals we have to deal with ourselves and with God as to how we adhere to this commandment. However, it doesn't negate the fact that the violation of this commandment is still part of the sin-system of our world. We've gone too far in the wrong direction. As I stated above, indeed the Sabbath is no longer truly the Sabbath.

The next six commandments have to do with our relationship to each other as humans. We have just seen how the first four commandments talk to our relationship to God; now it's man's turn. How does he fare up with his fellow man? Lets see.

#5 "Honor your father and your mother."

As youngsters growing up, there may be obvious times when we all have acted in disobedience to our parents. But even as adults, we may be guilty of not honoring our parents in various ways. When we don't care for their needs as they get elderly, this is not honoring to them. When we cast them aside as if they were never in our lives, this is not honoring to them. Ultimately, if we harbor any un-forgiveness towards our parents, perhaps related to any negative experiences we may have had in the home while growing up, this too is not honoring to them.

Is there such a thing as an abusive parent? Of course there is; we see it in the news all the time. Is there dysfunction and discord in homes today? All one needs to do is watch a daytime TV talk show to see how this is true. Is divorce rampant in our nation causing harsh break-ups in the home and sad child custody cases? It's a way of life in America.

All of these maladies in the home could lend themselves to how children grow up to not honor their father and their mother. As Christians, we must lay aside every sin that was committed against us by our parents and first forgive them, and second, attempt to meet their needs in whatever way possible.

There's more I could talk about with regards to this subject of forgiveness and honoring our parents, but my goal here is not to get into some deep psychological discussion about family dysfunctions, but rather to just show how this whole realm is part of the sin-system that we all live in each day. As part of my personal testimony later, I will show how the Lord dealt with me in this matter of honoring my parents, particularly my mother.

The next two commandments, #'s 6 & 7, have an interesting connection to one another. Let's see how.

#6 "You shall not kill"

There's no way to count the ways and amount of times that man has violated this law throughout time. The word "kill" here is taken from the ancient Hebrew word "ratsach" which really means to murder.

We know that even in the Bible there are times where killing is described as something that God allowed to happen, particularly between His children Israel and her enemies such as the Philistines. So it's almost as if certain types of killing is sanctioned, particularly in scenarios of war.

But then how does this relate to us individually? After all, I never killed, or better yet murdered, anyone. Jesus addresses this issue in Matthew chapter 5, verses 21 to 22: "You have heard that it was said to the people long ago 'Do not murder and anyone who murders will be subject to judgment.' But I tell you that anyone who is angry with his brother will subject to judgment." (NIV) So we see now with this commandment that there is a violation that takes place in the inward man, if not outwardly, that seems to be unavoidable. How many murders have we all committed, if only in our hearts, by being angry with our fellowman?

The next commandment has a similar situation.

#7 "You shall not commit adultery"

I used to think that this commandment referred only to a married person who cheated on his or her spouse. But then I read what Jesus said in Matthew 5: 27-28: "You have heard that it was said, 'Do not commit adultery'; but I tell you that anyone who looks at a woman lustfully has already committed adultery with her in his heart." (NIV)

So just as with the previous commandment, #6 on killing, here in this commandment, #7, we can't escape the violation of the heart, that is, what the inner man goes through, the lust of the eyes, ultimately, the lust of the flesh. It's one thing to admire the physical beauty of someone of the opposite sex, but it's quite another thing to dwell in our minds on sexual fantasies with that person. Who isn't guilty of this violation at some time in their life? I would venture to say no one, and depending on the environment you grew up in, some are more guilty than others.

I confess that I've broken this law countless number of times. I've gotten better over the years, but the temptation, the lust in my heart, always has a potential for re-appearing. More on this later in my personal testimony. For now, lets move on to our final 3 commandments.

#8 "You shall not steal"

This commandment is pretty straightforward, you might think; just don't take what doesn't belong to you. But if we dig a little deeper, we begin to see other ways that we have violated this commandment. Have you ever cheated on your taxes in some way, perhaps by including a deduction that really didn't exist? Guess what, you stole from the government. Even Jesus said to "Give to Caesar what is Caesar's..." (Matt. 22:21 NIV) Perhaps you're a home owner who, in order to make ends meet, rents an illegal room or apartment within your home and never claims the rent as income, much less informs any village official that you're doing this lest your property taxes get increased. I think <u>you know</u> what you're doing.

As a retired police officer, I could share numerous stories of what you might call traditional ways of stealing such as shop-lifting merchandise from retail stores, the stealing of money from persons right on the street via pick-pocketing or down right mugging. Other ways of stealing that one may not have thought of as stealing is the misdemeanor crime of "theft of service". In New York City, this crime occurs daily every time someone enters a subway station without paying the prescribed fare. They do this by hopping over a turnstile, or by sneaking in some unlocked gate, amongst other ways. As a side note, many a wanted criminal has been caught by the simple act of sneaking into a NY subway without paying the fare and not realizing that an under-cover police officer was waiting for them on the other side of the turnstiles. Every time someone tries to escape from paying for a taxi-cab ride, this too is theft of service. And lastly, if you enter a restaurant, order a meal, and then don't pay for it, that also is considered theft of service in NY.

While these examples just described above may seem like minor offenses, they're still examples of stealing. People just think they can get something for free that they're suppose to pay for. In reality, they are all in violation of the 8th commandment of God.

Are you getting the sense by now that these commandments are too convicting as well as impossible to totally adhere to? Welcome to the human race. Hopefully by the end of this book, if not by the end of this chapter alone, you will see the need for Jesus to "save" you.

#9 "You shall not bear false witness against your neighbor"

Once again, we have a pretty straightforward command here - don't lie. Be truthful in all you do. Have you never told a lie either about yourself or about someone else? Only you can answer that question. But consider this, lying only cheats our self. It shows something about our personality; it shows that we're not real with ourselves or with others. If we can't be honest in all of our affairs with others, how can we be honest with God? Just in human terms alone, I believe if one isn't true to himself nor to others he or she relates to, then that person isn't a true man or woman.

Lastly, #10 "You shall not covet your neighbor's house; (or)... your neighbor's wife"

To covet means to secretly desire something. In the context here, it's like we're saying to God that we're not satisfied with what we have or even with what He's blessed us with; we want what someone else has. It's more than just keeping up with the Jones' next door. It's envying them. It's craving what they have. It becomes our total focus, an obsession, almost our god. It can go hand in hand with stealing if we let it get that far; it can even go hand in hand with adultery if we let it get that far regarding our neighbor's wife.

In the Old Testament, David violated this commandment when he coveted Bathsheba. He sent her husband out to the front lines in a battle with one of Israel's enemies where he was killed, and then he, David, took Bathsheba for himself. (2 Samuel 11) Do you see the connection here to at least two other commandments we've already discussed?

Breaking It Down

When we break it down, the ten commandments are really divided into two commandments, as Jesus states in Matthew 22, verses 37 to 40: "You shall love the Lord your God with all your heart, and with all your soul, and with all your mind. This is the great and first commandment, and the second is like it, you shall love your neighbor as yourself. On these two commandments depend all the law and the prophets." (RSV) We've already seen this division in our look at the ten commandments as a whole. As we saw, the first four commandments deal with our relationship with God, and the next six commandments deal with our relationship with each other.

True love, not romantic love or "eros" love, as the Greeks call it, doesn't look for ways to hurt someone. This is the essence of the commandments; we <u>should</u> love God, and we <u>should</u> love our fellow man. But as we've seen, we fall short of this true love in our very nature each and every day. Martin Luther puts it this way: "The law says 'thou shalt not kill'. Its whole urging is directed towards what I am to do. It says: thou shalt love God with all thy heart and thy neighbor as thyself. Thou shalt not commit adultery, not swear, and not steal. And then it speaks out thus: see that you have lived or are now living according to what I command you to do. When you have reached this point, you will find that you do not love God with your whole heart as you should, and you will be forced to confess: O my God, I have not done what I should; I have not kept the law, for neither did I love thee from my heart today, nor will I do so tomorrow. I make the same confession year after year that I have failed to do this or that. There seems to be no end to this confessing of my trespasses. When will there be an end of this? When shall I find rest unto my soul and be fully assured of divine grace? You will ever be in doubt; tomorrow you will repeat your confession of today...."1

If that doesn't give you a clear picture of man's condition, I don't know what does.

To make matters worse, the letter of James gives us an interesting statement: "For whoever keeps the whole law but fails in one point has become guilty of all of it." (James 2:10) Talk about no way out.

The Gospel Again

The way out is through the sacrificial death of Jesus Christ. There is no other way. Moses is not the way. He was an instrument of God to bring forth the law which only condemns us. Even Paul said " ...I would not have known what sin was except through the law..." (Romans 7:7 NIV) Other religious figures are also not the way: Mohammed is not the way, Buddha is not the way, Rev. Moon is not the way, the Pope is not the way, no canonized saint is the way; and if you happen to be Roman Catholic, this may come as a shock to you at first, but even the Virgin Mary is not the way! Only Jesus, the promised Messiah of the Old Testament, is the way out of this mess called the sin of man.

Does this seem exclusive? Well yes it is. But at the same time, it's open to any and all regardless of one's nationality, of one's economic status, of one's ethnicity. All are welcome.

Before we move on, let me give another quote from a 19th century theologian by the name of Dr. C.F.W. Walther. He writes in his book "The Proper Distinction Between Law & Gospel" the following: "We see that the law was not revealed to us to put that notion into our heads that we can become righteous by it, but to teach us that we are utterly unable to fulfill the law. When we have learned this, we shall know what a sweet message, what a glorious doctrine, the gospel is and shall receive it with exuberant joy."2

Work Out Your Salvation

If everything I've written here up to this point is true, then how am I to live? Am I free to do whatever I want since I'm incapable of keeping the law anyway? Simply speaking the answer to that one is no. But the answer is much deeper than that. If you think this way, that is, that you can do whatever you want because God will forgive you anyway, and you know that you can't fulfill the law, so why try, then you missed something. What you missed is the whole concept of what Jesus talks about in the gospel of John, chapter 3, and that is the concept of being born again.

It's not my goal to get into a deep theological discussion here on what it means to be born again. But speaking plainly, it all boils down to where my heart is with God. When I come to that place in my life where I admit that I'm a sinner, I next confess my sin to the Lord and ask for forgiveness through the shed blood of Jesus; I then ask Jesus to come into my life in a new way, to be the Lord and savior of my life, this is when I become born again. Needless to say, there has to be a sincerity in this whole process. Anyone can go through the motions, say all the right things, and just pretend to be a born again believer. Unless there is a heart change, a heart transplant if you will, in the spiritual sense, then it's not genuine and a true repentance has not taken place. Sometimes, unfortunately this change in a person's life only comes after they've hit rock bottom in their particular circumstances. It's when a person <u>hasn't</u> hit the bottom of the heap yet in his or her life that they think they still have a little more time to play the field, and thus put God on the shelf until they need Him again the next time. They haven't reached the end of their rope yet in life; there's a little slack left in their rope, so God is really not needed at that moment in their lives'.

When I graduated from Hunter College in 1977, I believe the Lord led me to go work in the ministry of Teen Challenge, a Christian-oriented rehabilitation program for men and women with life controlling problems such as drug addiction and other issues. It wasn't long after entering that ministry that I saw two types of people who would come into the program. The first type of person was "real", that is, he or she had hit that bottom pit in their life and were truly ready for Christ to come in and make a change. The second type of person were what we called "gamers". These guys and gals played the game of "going along with the program", usually because they were mandated by some court to either enter a program, or go to jail for some crime they committed. For them, they hadn't reached their end-point yet, thus, they weren't ready to receive to Christ. As a side note, and this isn't intended as criticism against Teen Challenge, but there was a third category of person in that ministry. It was the workers, some of whom attended well-known Bible schools. Some, not all, interns from Bible Schools were heavy into legalism. They knew all the right things to say, all the Christian jargon, but they couldn't identify with someone down in the dumps. It got so bad sometimes, so mechanical that I thought everyone who came out of Bible school was a robot. It reminded me of some churches I visited over the years where heavy restrictions were placed on its members, restrictions on what kind of clothes to wear, never being allowed to watch television, never being allowed to dance, and all these things as if they had something to do with a person's salvation.

1978 : Yours truly in front of the original Teen Challenge Center in Brooklyn, NY - the ministry to drug addicts & people with other life controlling problems, founded by the Rev. David Wilkerson in the early 1960's. Intense spiritual warfare occurred there on a daily basis. I sometimes thought it was harder being there than on any foreign mission field.

So what does a genuine conversion experience look like? God puts a new desire in my heart. That new desire is to want to please God in anyway I can; that new desire is to want to do the things that I know that God wants me to do like truly loving Him and truly loving my neighbor as my self. All this is not out of obligation, but because I want to and because I know it pleases God.

Is there scripture to back this up? Certainly. In Jeremiah, God gives us the first clue as to what a true believer would look like. In chapter 31, starting at verse 31, God speaking through the prophet Jeremiah says, "Behold the days are coming...when I will make a new covenant with the house of Israel...I will put my law within them and I will write it upon their hearts..." (Jeremiah 31:31-34)

Herein lies the key; God makes a new pact with us, a new covenant. When we come in true repentance to the Lord, He puts that new <u>want to</u>, that new desire in our hearts to truly follow Him.

Are we perfect then? Only in our spirits' are we perfect. In our human flesh, we still have to let the sin nature die daily. It's a process. We are shown the way to live all throughout the New Testament. After we confess our sins, we're to repent of them, i.e. don't turn back to them like a dog who returns to its own vomit. We're to pray constantly, i.e. all the time (I Thessalonians 5:17); we're to study the word of God so that we may be equipped to quench the fiery darts of the devil (II Timothy 2:15 KJV); we're never to neglect to have fellowship with other believers for this is how we encourage one another, and even correct and learn from one another (Hebrews 10:25). Through all of this, hopefully, we become mature and put aside the milk of an infant that we initially fed ourselves on and replace it with more substantial meat (Hebrews 5:13-14).

Ultimately, as Paul says, we are to "work out our salvation with fear and trembling". (Philippians 2:12) Why is this? The answer is in the next verse, vs. 13: "For God is at work in you, both to will and to work for His good pleasure." Another reason that we should engage in those activities that enhance our spiritual growth, like the verses mentioned above on praying and studying the Bible suggest we do, is because we are involved in a spiritual warfare. The Apostle Peter encourages us in his first letter to "Be self-controlled and alert. Your enemy the devil prowls around like a roaring lion looking for someone to devour. Resist him, standing firm in the faith..." (I Peter 5:8-9) NIV And of course, Paul tells us in Ephesians that "..our struggle is not against flesh and blood, but against the rulers, against the authorities, against the powers of this dark world and against the spiritual forces of evil in the heavenly realms." (Ephesians 6:12) NIV

Make no mistake, we are all vulnerable to a fall, especially if we are not diligent in our walk. Later in this book, I expound a little on my fall. Thankfully, John tells us in his first epistle the following: "If we claim to be without sin, we deceive ourselves and the truth in not in us. If we confess our sins, He is faithful and just and will forgive us our sins and purify us from all unrighteousness." (I John 1:8-9) NIV

So if you think that you can live anyway you want even as a believer, guess what, you still have missed the mark. You don't have a clear focus yet on what it means to be a believer. You can escape the blessings that God has for you. It even becomes questionable whether or not you are a believer in the first place. Ultimately, only you and God know the answer to that one.

As we reviewed the gospel, we saw that Christ paid for our sins through His shed blood on Calvary's cross. But the message doesn't end there for we know that He also rose from the grave on the third day. If that event didn't take place, i.e. if He didn't rise from the dead, then I think it would be feasible to say as Paul did in I Corinthians 15:32b, "If the dead are not raised, 'Let us eat and drink, for tomorrow we die.'" (NIV) Without the resurrection, there would be no purpose to our faith and all of our works would be for naught. But if we agree that indeed Christ did rise from the dead, then as Paul says in that same chapter of I Corinthians, we should "come back to (our) senses..., and stop sinning." (15:34)

I close this chapter with one last passage of scripture from Paul. He says in his letter to the Ephesians, chapter 2 beginning at verse 8, "For by grace you have been saved through faith; and this is not your own doing, it is the gift of God - not because of works, lest any man should boast." Many Christians end the quote there when talking to people about God's grace. In reality, we should all contemplate what Paul says next, beginning with vs. 10: "For we are His workmanship, created in Christ Jesus for good works, which God prepared beforehand, that we should walk in them." (RSV)

My encouragement to you is don't miss the mark. Look to Him for how you should live.

Notes

1 Dr. C.F.W. Walther, <u>The Proper Distinction Between Law & Gospel</u> (St. Louis, Mo: Concordia Publishing House) p.22

2 Ibid, p.62

III

The Sin System

So far in this work, I have tried to focus on man's condition of sin, that is, the sin nature that dwells inside of him and how through God's grace we are saved through the shed blood of Jesus. I now want to focus on what are some of the effects of sin in our world.

John makes an interesting statement in his first epistle, chapter 2, beginning at vs. 15. He says "Do not love the world or the things in the world. If anyone loves the world, the love of the Father is not in him. For all that is in the world, the lust of the flesh and the lust of the eyes and the pride of life, is not of the Father but is of the world." (RSV)

At first glance, this passage could be highly mis-understood. John here is not saying that everything in the world, the physical beauty of the earth, the majesty of sun-rises and sun-sets, the glory of the stars and the moon at night are all evil. This is what the gnostics of Paul's time would have us to believe, that is that everything in the physical realm is all evil. Different Bible commentaries tell us that Paul tries to address this false doctrine in his first letter to Timothy. Indeed, even in the first book of the Bible, Genesis, we're told that after God created the world, He said it was good.

To the gnostics, however, only that which was of the spirit-world was good. Anything that was physical including the earth, human flesh, even human institutions such as government and laws were considered to be evil. Even marriage and sex fell into that evil category for the gnostics.

Throughout the years, we've seen the unfortunate results of believing in similar philosophies such as the gnostics believed in. Our generation has seen numerous cults that have led many people astray, some with dire consequences. In the 1970's, a pastor named Jim Jones led over 900 people in his congregation to commit suicide after leading them on a trip to Gyanna. Other groups have believed that they should separate themselves from the rest of the world and stay totally within a "Christian" community, sort of like a Christian commune. Any contact with the "outside" world was considered to be wrong.

So getting back to the context of our discussion, what is John talking about in his epistle? The answer is partially contained within the verse itself, the lust of the eyes and the pride of life. In our look at the ten commandments, we saw how lust causes us to sin against our fellow man; we saw how pride causes us to think as if we are gods and can do anything we choose to do. But there's more to this passage in John's epistle than meets the eye. John is saying that we are not to love the world system which is a system of sin.

Some Examples

What are some examples of this world system, or sin-system as I call it? The examples are many and varied. They show the imperfection of man and of the world he has created for himself.

We should first look at a particular verse of scripture that has a direct link to the sin system of our world. The verse is found in Paul's first letter to Timothy, chapter 6, verse 10; and it reads, "For the love of money is the root of all evils; it is through this craving that some have wandered away from the faith and pierced their hearts with many pangs." (RSV) Note that Paul isn't saying here that money in itself is evil, but rather it is the love of money that is evil. From this, it shouldn't be hard to see how this love of money enhances the problems of our world.

From a law enforcement perspective, I can tell you that it's been my experience that almost all crime in some form or fashion revolves around money, or should I say the lack of it. One small example illustrates this well, I believe. Robbery, drugs, and prostitution are crimes that of course all have their connection to money. These crimes are also inter-connected with one another. Lets see how; a woman may be addicted to drugs. In order for that woman to support her drug habit, she enters the world of prostitution. When the opportunity affords itself, the woman may rob her unsuspecting customer, or "John" as he's called in police circles, of more money than he was intending to pay the prostitute for her services. In addition to this, the element of homocide could be added to the mix. If the customer of a prostitute is mentally disturbed, he may murder the prostitute. Thus, from a criminological point of view, it's clear to see how the love of money is indeed part of the sin-system of our world.

Poverty

Poverty is an example of the sin-system of our world. At the risk of sounding like a socialist, which I'm not, I find it amazing that in our 21st century, poverty still exists in our world. To think that within our own hemisphere of North America, people go to bed hungry each night is beyond my comprehension. Of course, there are many causes of poverty in an individual's life, and there may be various inter-related factors. Sometimes, there is a lack of opportunity to advance in education. This in turn leads to low levels of income via some meanial employment. The longer one stays in this situation, the harder it becomes to advance up the economic ladder. Now if the person in this bracket has a family, perhaps with more children on the way, the chances of <u>ever</u> advancing becomes even harder. If a person in this category becomes desperate, they might resort to the criminal life to make ends meet, whether it be through engaging in the drug trade, prostitution and /or robbery - once again back to the three main crimes of inner city life.

In comes the government with various programs to help those in this economic condition. Some of these helps are in the form of educational grants and scholarships. For others, it may be what we used to call "welfare" or subsides to help families with no means of advancement. Now these programs seem to work, and they do for some. For others, the programs become something to abuse and to cheat on. Needless to say, throughout the years we have seen great strides in combating poverty, even though poverty does continue.

One might raise the question of whether or not poor people are in sin, that is, is it their sin which causes them to be poor. Obviously, an individual's choices and actions in life <u>can</u> contribute to whether or not they remain in the realm of poverty. For example, an unwed teenager who allows herself to get pregnant and has no means of support outside of her parent or parents has great potential for being in poverty for some time to come. Did that teenager sin in her actions? I think we can all agree the answer is yes. Can God still bless the child who is born from this action? The answer here is also yes. Even the mother in repentance can be blessed by God. In fact, with all sin, in true repentance there <u>is</u> forgiveness, but the consequences of our actions remain.

So again, are all people who are in poverty in sin? No more than anyone else is in sin. Individual people make individual choices. There are godly people who are in poverty just as there are intentional sinners who are in poverty. However, it would seem that the sin-system of certain crimes does thrive more in lower economic environments than in other kinds of environments.

The Philosophy of More

Related to why certain crimes seem to thrive more in certain environments is the philosophy of more. Each day we are bombarded through the media of tv, magazines, billboards, etc. of the "need" to have more. We have to have more of this and more of that. It could be anything; more clothes, more jewelry, more appliances, more cars. You name it and we just have to have more of it. The implication from the media is that you won't be happy till you acquire these things. After all, the people in the advertisements are always smiling, so they <u>must</u> be happy.

Without a true identity of one's self, without a true focus of who you really are as a person and as a human being, you can get trapped into thinking that you have a low self worth simply because you don't possess all the things that the sin-system of the philosophy of more tells you that you should have.

The result of this for those in the low economic status of poverty may be to engage in criminal activity just so they <u>can</u> get all the things that the media says they should have in order to be happy. For other people in the working world, they may begin the process of slowly killing themselves by working tons of over-time so that they too can acquire those things in the category of "gotta have that", or "gotta have more" in order to be happy. These people may spend little time with their family resulting in other problems down the line.

Real Estate

Related to the philosophy of more is the world of real estate. Our urban areas never seem to stop building high-rises, sometimes in locations where smaller more intimate dwellings used to exist. In New York, just when you thought an area should be done with any kind of construction, along comes a demolition crew to knock something down and then begin building something bigger than what was there before. It's a wonder that there are any open spaces left in New York. Maybe some day, even the parks will disappear.

All this leads to the impersonal life style of our urban environments; people living on top of one another, not really knowing any of their neighbors; just co-existing as they lock themselves in at night in their voluntary prisons called apartments. Loneliness thrives in high-rise apartment buildings despite the number of people actually living there.

Past sociological studies have shown that urban environments really only cater to middle-aged working people with no families present at their living space. Another words, those middle aged working people with no families had no problems living in urban environments, particularly in high rises, because their sole focus in life was on their work. They come and go as they please and are able to fend for themselves.

Contrast this to people with young children, the same studies showed that these people faced danger in the streets of urban environments. The danger was found to be in the form of vehicular traffic, physical concerns such as something as simple as a falling object from a building, and lastly, the criminal element.

The elderly in urban environments were found to be in worse shape, according to the studies. They face the same dangers that the families with young children do, with the added factor that they're not as strong as they once were. If a mechanical problem happens in a high rise building such as the elevators going out of service, or even when an electrical black-out occurs, the elderly are the first ones to be trapped.

What am I saying by all of this? I'm attempting to paint a picture of how the sin-system of our world has permeated practically every aspect of life. Was man ever meant to live this way, in an impersonal, overly mega-sized urban environment? Personally, I believe not. It's a funny thing. In the Bible, the first book of Genesis gives us the account of Cain killing his brother Abel. Then do you know what happens next? Cain, after being confronted by the Lord for what he did, flees with his wife and builds a city (Gen. 5:17). Imagine that, the first city built by a murderer!

Real Estate & Money

I couldn't end my discussion on real estate without briefly talking about its connection to money. Again, using my home town of New York as an example, it's a wonder how anyone could afford to live anymore in NY. The whole gamut of real estate, everything from property taxes to just general rent has gone beyond anyone's imagination. The city itself has become a place where you're either rich or you're poor. There's no such thing as a middle class anymore.

It's amazing to see a luxurious high rise building go up on any given street, and then to recognize that not too far away, maybe a difference of only a few blocks, exist a group of projects where poor and low income people reside. Even what were once industrial areas with numerous factories have turned into exclusive neighborhoods where "lofts" now exist that the common blue-collar person could never afford. Indeed, places like Manhattan have seemed to be reserved only for the well-to-do of our society. In the end, it's all about money.

The priorities of our world have gotten out of wack. The money makers of the real estate world don't care who they affect. They'll build another sports stadium before they'll build an affordable housing development, or before they'll build a school, or a hospital. This is how it is in the sin-system of our world. Money rules!

Am I saying by all of this that I believe that prosperity is bad? Not necessarily. What I <u>am</u> saying, however, is that greed is bad, and unfortunately, I believe greed is the thing that rules men's hearts in our world today.

Before I move on to discuss other areas, I want to close this chapter with a concept you may or may not have ever thought of before. When Adam and Eve sinned in the garden of Eden, the Lord told Adam "Cursed is the ground because of you; in toil you shall eat of it all the days of your life;..." (Gen. 3:17) So because of this, man works each day in order to survive. He <u>has</u> to; he has no choice. There's no way of knowing what life would have been like if Adam and Eve had totally obeyed God and had not sinned. All we do know is that we have to work. Man has turned work into a struggle. Because of greed, we kill ourselves as well as each other in order to get by. It's almost as if we're never satisfied. In the environment I grew up in, it was called "hustling". Life is nothing but a hustle. Each day was a hustle to make a buck, to make ends meet, in essence, to "get over" till the next day. <u>This</u> is all part of the sin-system of our world of which John tells us not to love.

IV

The Sin System
(Continued)

I want to move on to other areas in talking about this so-called sin-system of our world, but permit me to reiterate in general what I'm trying to say in this book. We live in a corrupted world. The world is corrupt because it is filled with corrupt people. The world is imperfect because <u>we</u> are imperfect. We saw in chapter 2 how we are all in this predicament called sin, unable to live up to the standards that God originally intended for us, and in need of a savior.

An Example From Police Work

After my time and my employment in the ministry of Teen Challenge had come to an end, I became a police officer with the New York City Transit Police Department. (The Transit Police Dept. was an independent agency before its merger with the regular City Police Dept. in 1995 by order of then Mayor Rudi Guiliani. The Transit Police's main function was patrolling the NYC subway system.) I worked for 20 years as a NY cop, a job I thoroughly enjoyed. The stories of "the job", as we call it, are enough for a separate book. But now I want to exhibit here in this work at least a couple of examples of how even in police work, there is an occasional unfairness, there is an occasional corruption both towards the public and towards the police themselves. It too, as far as I'm concerned, is part of the sin-system of our world. Police work is like a microcosim of life itself; wherever there is an injustice, wherever there are people hurting, and conversely wherever there is some good that is done, the police experience it all.

The first thing that everyone should know is that police work is not like it's portrayed on television. Everyone is not involved in deadly shoot-outs with bad guys on a daily basis. Car chases, like the kind you see happening from time to time on California highways, occur only once in a while; in fact depending on where a police officer specifically works, his or her day could be quite boring. In my time "on the job", I went through the whole gamut, everything from highly intense moments of walking into robberies in progress, riots in the streets (eg. the Crown Heights riots in Brooklyn, NY during the late 80's), to just calm, nothing happening type of days. The examples I want to give here now may seem trivial in comparrison to everything else that police experience, but I hope you can see what I'm trying to say is related to the subject and context of this work.

Just as retail businesses measure their productivity by how much money is actually made through the sales of a given product, or the stock market measures how the world is engaged in the buying and selling of different items, so the police department also measures its productivity by how it deals with crime. Every now and then, a little controversy would rise up regarding whether or not the police department engages in a so-called "quota system" of so many tickets being given out and so many arrests that were to be made during the course of a month. Now, if you're a law abiding citizen, your first reaction might be that you're glad that the police are out there effecting arrests and giving out tickets to "bad people". After all, that's what they deserve for breaking the law, no matter how minor or major the offense.

Well, here's how the quota system really works. For each month in a calendar year, the police department measures its activity, i.e. how many arrests were made by its members for any given number of crimes, and also any other activity such as the simple act of the giving out of summonses, or tickets as they're commonly called. These sums are then compared to how the department did in the same month of the previous year. So for example, if a particular police precinct gave out X amount of summonses in the month of March one year, then in the following year in that same month of March gave out less summonses, the higher ups of the department would start to get a little nervous. While these higher ups would say that they're just measuring the department's productivity, it's really seeing how they can justify their existence if the numbers aren't where they're "suppose" to be. After all, each ticket generates currency for the city. If the numbers aren't there, then neither is the currency.

This process then translates down to the common foot soldier, i.e. the patrol officer being told to "get the activity up." Hence, the average Joe Citizen has the potential for getting a violation summons for something as simple as drinking a can of beer while sitting on the front stoop of his own residence, and this after a hard days' work!

During my time on the job as a police officer, I saw the evolution of the quota system happen before my eyes. When I first joined the NYC Transit Police in 1982, the subways were literally out of control. All kinds of crimes and offenses were occurring on a daily basis, everything from armed robberies both on board trains and on stations, to assaults, to just general mayhem and various quality of life violations which really made traveling on the subways an annoyance, not to mention dangerous in some locations, especially at night. Then a funny thing happened. With passing time, and the increase in man-power, it was like someone had come down into the bowels of the NY subways with a mop and just cleaned everything up. Those persons that cleaned everything up were us, the NYC Police Officer. We did this with pride because we knew we were only doing the right thing. There was no problem making arrests or giving out tickets for minor violations because it was all out there for the taking. But here's the thing that happened. One day, everyone noticed that crime in the subways was down, I mean it had dropped dramatically. Now you might think, we won the war; the fight was over. Not so. The higher ups of the department kept pushing and pushing the police to "generate" more activity. If you could believe this, there were days where my partners and I literally saw not one violation or offense occur over an 8 and a half hour period. The supervisors, some of whom came out on the road with us, saw what was happening as well. It was true, crime had dropped dramatically, not only in the subways, but on the streets of NY as well. Even the movies spoke to this condition. An example is Spike Lee's movie "Summer of Sam" where in the beginning of the movie, NY Daily News columnist Jimmy Breslin talks to how crime in NY dropped throughout the 1980's and 90's, all after such notorious crimes like the "Son of Sam" murders were finally solved.

So what were the higher ups of the department to do? How were the members of certain specialized units in the police department going to continue to justify their existence and keep the funding coming in if they weren't actually doing anything? One answer was to invent more violations. Things that were formerly over-looked, such as a homeless man sleeping on a park-bench, were now hit with tickets and in some cases even arrests. If a homeless person doesn't have an official address, how can you give him a ticket? The solution was to just use one of the many homeless-shelter addresses. Of course, no one ever expected any of these tickets to ever get paid by the individual recipient, but now it didn't matter. Where the department in the past may have been concerned about the quality of tickets being given out by its members, now it was just concerned about the quantity.

Another example of the numbers game which I personally experienced during my career was when I worked for the Truant Squad. This is the unit that would pick up kids during school hours who were playing hookie. In NY, many kids used to come down to the Times Square area to go to the movies or video arcades instead of going to school. While patrolling around in uniform and in marked police vans so that one would have any mistake that we were the police, we would round up dozens of kids at a time and bring them to one centrally located school in the mid-town Manhattan area. There, members of the Board of Education would have their own officials present to process each child who was brought in. Each child was simply logged in and then told to report back to his or her own school. Sometimes parents were notified as well as the child's school which he or she attended.

Here again, as police officers, those of us who worked in the truant squad thought we were doing something good, something noble, something positive to keep kids on the right track. But I began to notice that the Board of Ed. really didn't seem too concerned about whether or not a child actually did report to his or her school after being picked up by the truant squad. I enquired from Board of Ed. officials why this was. Their response to me was that just as long as the truants were officially logged in as being picked up, that's all that counted. What they did after that didn't matter. The more kids that were picked up, the more money that was generated by city government earmarked for truancy!

Do you see what I'm trying to say by these examples given above? It's all about money. There's no real concern for who gets hurt, or helped for that matter. It was how much activity can we generate to justify our existence. Gun-ho cops who would try to keep up with the demands of the numbers game would sometimes get into trouble. Civilian complaints against police officers would rise up as different cops tried to please their bosses and do their jobs. Unfortunately, even more serious events such as police shootings of unarmed civilians could sometimes be traced back to how those members were just trying to do their assigned jobs and keep the activity up, especially in plain-clothes details.

As a side note, you might wonder how did most cops deal with this constant pressure from our bosses to produce more activity. The answer was simple. It came in the form of two words we would always say to our supervisors, "Yes sir". That's all you really had to do when confronted by a boss to bring your activity up; just say the magic words "yes sir". If you tried to argue your point that nothing is happening out there, you were marked as a mal-content officer. The point was to never argue; just go out there and do your best. If you saw something go down, you would take any action that was necessary; and conversely, if you saw nothing, then you did nothing. No one was able to prosecute you for just being out because in point of fact, you <u>were</u> doing your job, even if it was only in the sense of being a deterrent to the bad guy.

There is more I could talk about in this subject, like how some police unfortunately dealt with job pressures through such things as alcohol and drugs, and even suicide, but I want to move on to other topics concerning greed, again, all pointing to the sin-system of our world.

Other Areas of Greed

Did you ever notice over past years how there seemed to be an increase in television commercials which advertised different law firms willing to fight for you if you've been involved in some sort of accident? It came to the point where people starting suing other people for almost anything under the sun. It sort of reminds me of a funny skit I saw once years ago on NBC's "Saturday Night Live" program. In the skit, the late Phil Hartman plays an attorney working for the law firm of "Green & Fazio". He encourages anyone who thinks they have a basis for a law-suit to give them a call. One of the lines in the skit was, "were you involved in an accident? Did you just witness an accident? Even if you weren't involved in the accident, you may be entitled to compensation just for being in the area at the same time!" Then, in the skit, they would cut to people on the street who tell of how Green & Fazio had helped them. One of the actresses on the program at that time, Ellen Cleghorne, would be seen exiting a beautiful limo and wearing a mink coat and exclaimed "I never thought that throwing myself in front of that subway train would be my ticket to financial independence." I laughed till I cried on that one.

As a Transit cop in the 1980's, I saw how scenarios like the one described above were almost true to life. Each year, New York's public transportation company, the MTA (Metropolitan Transportation Authority), would face countless lawsuits against it by people who claim they were somehow injured while traveling on either a bus or a train. Occassionally, I would get calls to respond to such incidents to take a police report. When I would arrive on the scene, there would be no sign of any accident or injury to anyone present. In every case, no matter what the circumstances, the MTA would eventually pay out a certain sum. It became so easy to sue the MTA over something so frivolous that everyone started to say that the initials "MTA" spelled backwards is "ATM"! Indeed, money rules in the hearts of many.

Drugs

The illegal drug trade of course is all about money. I'm going to make a controversial statement at this juncture which you might or might not agree with. It is my personal belief and conviction that the Federal Gov't. allows a certain percentage of illegal drugs to enter the country each year. There are two possible reasons for this. First, it enhances the economy, and second, it keeps certains groups of people under control.

Back in the 1990's, the ABC TV program "20-20" did a segment where they showed how the Federal Gov't. allowed a portion of drugs from Columbia, South America to enter our country through Florida for the purposes of tracing where exactly the drugs ended up. Just think of this for a moment. How many people took those drugs? How many people may have died from those drugs? These questions were not answered on that particular program. Only one thing was clear, the drugs were allowed in to our country by our own government.

Is there or has there ever been a true war on drugs? I think it's clear that there has never been a war, at least not in the traditional sense of how we think of war, on the drug trade. Local muncipalities fight drugs all the time. Some of the most dangerous assignments that under-cover police officers engage in is in the world of drug trafficking. An under-cover nacaotics officer truly puts his or her life on the line when they infiltrate groups who are engaged in the drug trade. Throughout the years, the police have lost some good men in "buy & bust" operations where something went wrong. Truly, when a nacaotics officer leaves home in the morning and kisses his wife good-bye, it very well could be for the last time.

So again, the question is does the Federal Gov't. really fight against the influx of illegal drugs into our nation? Do you think that if there was a military confrontation against the drug trade the same way our military has fought over in Iraq or in other so-called traditional wars that there would ever be drugs on our streets? I would tend to think not. But here's something to consider; if for example all of Columbia's drug farms were wiped off the face of the map, what would happen to Columbia's economy? I like to suggest that maybe one reason our government doesn't <u>really</u> fight drugs, at least not all the way as in a traditional war, is because of the severe consequences to not only the economies of foreign governments, but also to our own economy. After all, drug dealers handle big money. It trickles down to the low -level street dealer who, because he has no other way to support himself, now has money to buy all the things that he needs to survive and get by. Of course, the big guys are the ones who buy the fancy cars, nice clothes, and even perhaps gorgeous homes. Who would want this to end? The user of drugs, and the user's family are the ones who suffer and pay the price.

Indeed, the sin-system of greed reigns supreme in the world of illegal drug trafficking.

<u>War</u>

In a certain sense, war, the real kind of war which involves military confrontations between countries, is also part of the sin-system of our world. How can I say this, you might ask. Well, two things are for certain regarding war. First, in a monetary sense, the only ones who benefit financially from war are members of the military industrial complex. Their lobby in Washington D.C. is big and thus, they have a large influence in the politics of our country.

The second reason war is part of the sin-system of our world is a spiritual one. The enemy of us all, Satan, loves war. Why is this? Every war has maximum potential for loss of life, hence, maximum potential for more souls that are lost for eternity. This is exactly what the author of death wants. The more military conflicts that exist in our world, the more Satan gains in numbers of lives lost.

Is there any such thing as a justified war? I believe that throughout time, there <u>have</u> been so-called justified wars. In my mind, World War II was probably the last really justified conflict that we were ever involved in. Conversely, there have also been many unjust wars. At the time that I am writing this, our nation is involved in a war in Iraq that was started under highly questionable circumstances. As a side note, when 9-11 happened, I was on duty that fateful morning. When I saw the results of the attack that day on New York's World Trade Center, and how we lost so many members of the department, including a member of my unit, Police Officer Ray Suarez, I thought to my self that anyone who is found to be responsible for this should definitely be dealt with in a crushing blow. There's only one problem, to this day, there has been no proof that Iraq had anything to do with 9-11.

Nonetheless, the war in Iraq received tremendous support in the beginning by many in politics, even by some in the evangelical community including a well known preacher from Texas. I was never sure, however, that we made the right move going in there. The war has turned into another Vietnam, a no win and no way out situation.

The Sin System Of Our World

2001 : Two pictures from the tragedy of 9/11, taken by myself three days after the incident. Above, Firemen approach the destruction of # 7 World Trade Center at West Broadway & Barclay Sts. The next picture is a more close up view of that building.

The flames and smoke, not to mention the smell of death, lingered for months in lower Manhattan.

So again, the question becomes who is benefiting from this war? Did the Iraqi people benefit from the overthrow of Saddam? Perhaps in certain areas they have. Are the Iraqis benefiting from all of the strife between rival Muslim factions? The answer to that one should be obvious. I do know that at least two other parties <u>are</u> benefiting from a prolonged war in Iraq; they are the military industrial complex, and Satan. I leave it to you to be the judge of whether or not I'm telling the truth. All I can say is may God have mercy on us for the mistakes we have made as a nation.

V

Sex, Love and Marriage

If ever there was an area in our current society that is so fickle, so out of touch with God's perfect plan for man as far as relationships go, it's in the area of sex, love and marriage. It almost seems that not a week goes by where we don't hear or read about some famous personality, particularly in Hollywood, who is going through some marital breakup, or some illicit affair between married people and others.

Indeed, the gossip magazines and TV shows thrive on these kind of stories. Unfortunately, it seems that divorce in our country has become common place, not just in Hollywood, but everywhere, including in the church.

Divorce

As a youngster growing up in New York City, one thing was prevalent with almost everyone I was acquainted with, and that was that my closest friends' parents, including my own parents, had at some time in their lives', gone through a divorce. In fact, I'm not even sure that in those days any of us even knew what a so-called "normal" family was supposed to look like. I remember watching television shows like "Ozzie and Harriet", and "Father Knows Best" and "Leave It To Beaver", all of which had both parents present in the home, and how for the most part everyone in those homes of the

TV world seemed happy together. Why couldn't my home life look like that, I thought to myself.

As far as I knew, my biological father was never really married to my mother. They just met somewhere, only God knows where, had a relationship, and out I came. My father never lived with my mother and me. When I was 3 or 4 years old, my mother did get married to another man. From all recollections that I have, my step-father was good to me and to my mother. But then something happened; my mother and step father would constantly argue with one another. I even remember one physical fight between them. My reaction would be to constantly cry and to be afraid. Finally the day came, maybe when I was about 6 or 7, that my mother and step-father were divorced. It was back to just me and my mother living together in our Upper West Side apartment.

I will return to talking more about my personal testimony in a little while, but first, I just want to explore this concept of divorce further.

When I think back on all the heartache, all of the pain that divorce caused in me and in my mother, not to mention how I saw the same things happening in the lives of my friends whose parents had also went through a divorce, I believe I can say with certainty now that divorce is truly part of the sin-system of our world. Divorce can cause emotional scaring in children which may have negative consequences down the line with passing time.

A question that one might raise is should no one ever get divorced? I believe there are cases where divorce may be the only avenue out of a bad situation. Adultery and spousal abuse are just two examples. It doesn't negate the fact, however, that divorce is still a sin. Perhaps the marriage of the two individuals in the first place was a sin and should never have happened.

Unfortunately, many have gone into marriage not really being prepared for it, that is to say many have entered marriage with the wrong ideas about how it's going to be or should be, and some have entered marriage with all the wrong motives in the first place. For example, if one goes into marriage just to have "legal" sex, they're in for a rude awakening when the honeymoon is over and it's time to relate to one another in other areas.

In my mind, there's no question that the institution of marriage was ordained by God as recorded in the book of Genesis. At the same time, I believe it's questionable whether or not each and every <u>individual</u> marriage is ordained by God. For this one, however, I believe we'll never know the true answer this side of paradise, and I'm willing to submit that I could be wrong.

The Apostle Paul tells us in First Corinthians, chapter 7, in so many words that it's better to remain single than it is to marry. In fact, he encourages us to "remain" in the state in which we were called to the faith. Then he says another interesting fact; in verse 28, he states "…if you marry, you do not sin,…yet those who marry will have worldly troubles, and I would spare you that." (RSV) To me, if ever there was a right-on statement in the Bible, this is it.

I remember hearing the confession of two different young women who admitted in so many words during a home Bible study group that they each had married the particular men that they did out of rebellion against their own parents. In their respective stories, there was something about each husband's character that made the parents of the women warn them not to marry them. Each woman went ahead and married those men anyway. The result years later were unhappy marriages that for one led to separation and divorce after years of fighting in the courts; for the other, it led to her having an affair outside of her marriage. I never knew whatever happened to that second woman as I never saw her again.

So in this example just described above, where was the sin? Initially, I believe the sin was in their rebellion to their parents and getting married to someone that they probably should never have done so. Added to this next is the sin of divorce. Plus, for each case, there were children involved. Thus, we have a third element: the hurt caused to them.

It should be clear to everyone that the institution of marriage has suffered greatly in our society, not for one reason, not for two, or three reasons, but for multiple reasons. The cycle of sin continues to effect consequences down through time for which we're all guilty of not using wisdom in our life's choices. Yet despite this, thankfully there <u>are</u> still marriages that hold together.

Personal Testimony

I want to take time now to share with you some aspects of my personal testimony which hopefully will shed light on my own shortcomings and failures in relating to the opposite sex. This is not meant as an exercise in laying blame on others for my own sins, but rather my purpose is just to show the importance of having good role models in life. Where those models don't exist, there is always the potential for dangerous choices.

A few pages ago, I left off with my mother divorcing my stepfather, and it was back to just my mother raising me up by herself as we resided in our upper Manhattan apartment. As my mother had no skills and no means of financial support, she resorted to a life of prostitution. She would meet men at bars where she would hang out at, bring them home, and have sex for money with those men. From this, she developed a clientel of men who would come by our apartment regularly to have sex with her. Each time that this happened, my mother would force me to remain in my bedroom and would threaten me with a severe beating if I were to ever come out while she engaged in her trade. At other times throughout the course of a year, my mother would have wild drinking parties in our apartment. She even purchased one of those bar-tables to put right in the living room which would augment the atmosphere of making one think that they actually were in some bar in the street. Finally, there were times of wild sex orgies with various men, all the while as I mentioned above I would be forced to remain in my room and prohibited from coming out, not even to go to the bathroom. One other note; my mother would occasionally rent our apartment to other women who would have sex with men themselves for which my mother would get a portion of the payout from the men!

All throughout these times, my young heart was broken. I would cry out to God in the only prayers I knew from the Catholic Church hoping that some day all this would somehow come to an end. Another heart-breaking thing about everything that I experienced was that I believe my closest friends and their mothers' knew about everything that was happening in my home and the life-style that my mother was living. Thankfully, no one ever talked about it with me. Although legally, my mother could have very well been prosecuted for what she was doing, no one ever turned her in to the police. I think in those days, none of us, meaning my friends and myself, knew what to do. I also believe that my friends didn't want to embarrass me by letting me know that they knew about everything that was happening in my home. I truly don't know what my reaction would have been if they had said something to me.

(How This Relates)

So how does this sad tail of a dysfunctional home relate to the topic of this work? Growing up, I didn't know what true love looked like. I had no model of it in my home, nor in the homes of anyone closest to me. All I came to know was that women were something to be used for sex, something to be conquered, and then let go. Later in life, a spirit of lust would be manifested in me. Obviously, this isn't how God desires for anyone to live. This philosophy of life is truly part of the sin-system of our world.

As the years progressed and I got older, there were many positive experiences which I had outside of my home. My mother was still a prostitute, even into my high school years. By then, however, she had slowed down her activities. Gone were the days of wild parties in our apartment, but she still had her customers, most of whom by then would only come by when I wasn't around. As for me, I found escape from my home life by participating in sports at school, specifically track & field (a year round event, both indoors and out), and also I got hooked up with a rock and roll band for which I played the drums. I never took any lessons; it just came naturally to me. We would practice every Saturday for months. We then became good enough to play at different functions for which we even earned some money. They were genuinely fun times for me.

After graduating from high school, I entered Hunter College which is part of the City University of New York and had free tuition for its city residents at that time. Although I had received all of my education up until then in both Catholic grammar and high school, there was no way I could afford to attend any private or Catholic college. Thus, CUNY (the City University) was my only choice.

Besides this, in those days, you either entered college, or you were drafted into the Army to go fight in Vietnam. I didn't consider myself a pacifist, but somehow I thought going into college would be better for me than going into the Army against my wishes.

After completing my first year in college, I once again entered the world of running by joining my school's cross-country running team. A fellow runner on the team one day invited me to come check out a Christian fellowship that he was a part of on our college campus. The fellowship was part of a campus ministry known as Inter-Varsity Christian Fellowship. I attended their meetings for some time. Ultimately, it was through this ministry that one day I made a personal commitment to the Lord Jesus Christ. For the first time in my life, I believe my spiritual eyes had been opened to what the gospel message was really all about. I began to read the Bible which in all my years of Catholic upbringing I never did. I was to begin a new journey in life.

One aspect of my journey was that I saw how I needed to forgive my mother for the heart-ache she gave me due to her life style. I was only able to do this as I reflected on how God had forgiven me for all of my shortcomings, all of my failures, and all of the ways that I had hurt others. (Matt. 6:14)

1974 : Members of the Hunter College Cross-Country Track Team pose for a picture at Van Cortland Park in the Bronx, site of all cross-country races held in NY. I'm standing in the extreme left; my hair was wild in those days. Unfortunately, the fellow runner who led me to the Lord wasn't present for this picture.

I thought of how my mother must have been hurt when she was young, perhaps even abandoned by her own parents, whom by the way I never met. (Ironically, I only knew my biological father's side of the family even though he himself never lived with us.) Ultimately, I thought of how she herself never knew what true love looked like.

As she got older, my mother engaged in menial work; she was a waitress for a short time, she also engaged in child-care for other working mothers. She went to church a lot, even bringing the children she was baby-sitting along with her. Social service would move her around to different places to live. Her final residence was in a senior citizen high-rise in mid-town Manhattan, which conveniently was right around the corner from Dave Wilkerson's Times Square Church. I took it upon myself to bring her to that church for services at least a couple of times. She then started to attend on her own. I can't say that I ever asked her if she had accepted the Lord into her heart. But I believe I did plant a seed which I trust God watered in His timing.

I believe the Lord led me to honor her by starting to contribute financially to her in anyway and anytime that I could. I took care of some of her bills and just gave her money for food and other things. Finally, in April of 2006, my mother had passed away. Her story had thus ended.

Lust Reviewed

As we saw in an earlier chapter, the Apostle Paul tells us in his letter to the Ephesians, chapter 6 and verse 12 that "our struggle is not against flesh and blood, but against the rulers, against the authorities, against the powers of this dark world and against the spiritual forces of evil in the heavenly realms." (NIV)

From this verse, we see that there is a battle that is being waged, an unseen battle, one not visible to the naked eye. It is a battle for men's souls which is being fought on a daily basis. The spiritual forces of evil are out to get us anyway they can. Different geographical areas may have particular spirits that are on the attack, seeking whom they may devour. For example, places like Las Vegas and Atlantic

City may have a spirit of gambling that are attacking people who are addicted to that sort of thing. Places like Arizona and New Mexico may have a spirit of witchcraft and Satanism which in past times have been discovered to being practiced in certain desert areas. The dominating spirit of New York is greed and money. Of course, other spirits are also at work in large urban areas such as New York, but again, it would appear from all outward circumstances that indeed money is the main spirit at work here.

Back-tracking on my personal testimony, when I reflect on some of the things I engaged in as teenager, it became clear to me only later in life that a spirit of lust was prevalent in me and in my friends. Even before I had all of those positive experiences I spoke of earlier, such as my participating in sports in my high school, and my playing in a local rock and roll band, I had a distorted view of how to interact with girls. One example of this is how in the neighborhood where I grew up, my friends and I would attend numerous house parties. At these parties, all of us, guys and girls, would dance with each other to the top hit records of those days. Nothing wrong there, you might say. But then when it came to slow dancing, we had a dance that we called "the grind". It was something like right out of the movie "Dirty Dancing". Of course, we were doing that type of dancing long before that particular movie ever came out. Anyway, at the party, you would get a girl, hopefully the prettiest one in the group, and you would dance this slow dance with her in which you were practically feeling her up through your clothes. This was only the beginning for me of my fulfilling my lustful desires.

Jumping ahead, as I already spoke about, when I made a commitment to the Lord while in college, things for me started to change. I learned many new aspects of the scriptures and what it really means to be a Christian. I believe I was truly blessed with all that the Lord was doing with me. For a long time, I was celebate. I didn't date any young lady. I had no feelings for any lady, and this was ok by me at that time. I felt no pressure to be in any dating relationship. You might say I was satisfied as a single guy. After college, as I spoke of earlier, I went to work in a Christian ministry, Teen Challenge. My time there, just as with my time on the police force, holds enough stories for a separate book.

In the year 1982, I joined the New York City Transit Police Department. After going through a tough six month training period in the police academy, I felt like I was thrown into the lion's den when I was sent out on patrol for my first mid-night tour in the section of Manhattan known as Harlem. The only consolation was that unlike some of the other officers I graduated with, I was quite familiar with the neighborhood having grown up not too far from there, and also having gone to high school there. In a spiritual sense, however, it was like taking a giant step backwards in terms of growth.

As a native New Yorker, I thought I had seen it all, and knew it all about life in general. When I became a cop, I found this to not be true; there were things which I had never experienced before. I learned of so many ways that various crimes were committed each and every day. In the subways of NY, different types of sex crimes were prevalent, everything from sexual abuse by perverts who would take advantage of women on crowded trains, to men who would expose themselves, and even to men who would engage in homo-sexual acts at various locations. Other types of crimes such as robberies were also a daily occurrence. Pick-pockets were strong in the subways, particularly during the rush hours when the trains are the most crowded.

The point of all of this is that I had once again entered a new world. Whereas my spiritual eyes had become opened in a new way when I became a Christian, now, after joining the police department, my worldly eyes had become re-opened, if you will, to a world of decadence, a world of depravity, a world of despair, ultimately, a world of evil.

1982 : As a rookie Transit Police Officer, I worked many a tour during the mid-night hours riding the graffiti - covered New York City Subways. Truly, it was an interesting experience, to say the least.

I didn't stop going to church just because I became a cop, but I was now being bombarded on a daily basis with all sorts of temptations. The enemy knows where to hit us in our most vulnerable areas. For some cops, money was a big temptation. An example of this was in different drug raids that would take place. If ever there was a huge sum of money present in those raids, inevitably there would be reports later of portions of that money missing. I recall once being assigned to drive up to Harlem to a location where members of the warrant squad had made a pre-dawn raid on an apartment where different felons had been residing. My specific assignment was to take those arrested to the station house for processing. When I arrived at the location, the supervisor asked for volunteers to remain at the apartment until all the drugs and money that was found in the apartment could be counted and vouchered. As far as I recall, there was supposedly tens of thousands of dollars present in that apartment. I respectfully declined to stay; I just wanted to take the bodies (the bad guys) to the precinct and get out of there.

My weakness wasn't money. I soon came to see it was lust. I began to meet physically attractive women while at work. Depending on a particular assignment I would have, some places were easier to meet women than at other places. I discovered that some women were just naturally attracted to the uniform. For some other women, they just wanted to meet somebody who had a good job and with whom they could possibly get hooked up with in order to escape from their impoverished condition, a ticket out of the ghetto, as it were. With passing time, it only got worse for me. Everytime I met some good looking woman, I would take her phone number and try to make some arrangement to meet her someplace after work. These encounters wouldn't happen daily or even weekly sometimes, but they happened often enough. Mind you, all of this was in complete contrast to those years immediately following my making a personal commitment to the Lord as I've already explained. You might say that my becoming a cop was a step backwards, or at the very least, a step into the dark side.

When I met the woman I would eventually marry, even this encounter was out of lust. We went out on some dates, had an affair with one another, and then one day got engaged. Did I love this woman? Considering my background, I can only say that I wasn't sure what love, true love, looked like. I suppose I had a sense of what God's love looked like after all of my studying into the scriptures. Clearly this type of love, agape love, was exhibited on Calvary's cross over 2000 years ago. But as far as loving between humans goes, i.e. the romantic type of loving between the sexes, I believe I still had a warped view.

I had reached the age of 30 and had been a cop for over a year when I thought to myself, "if I don't get married now, when will I ever get married?". Despite numerous signs that I shouldn't get married, at least not at the time that I did, and not to the woman that I proposed to, I went ahead and did it anyway. It was doomed from the start. As I walked down the aisle, I knew in my heart that I was making a mistake. Truly, I was not in love, at least not the way a couple should be. The sad thing is that I don't even know why I went ahead with the whole thing.

I began to reason with myself that maybe there was something subconsciously going on inside of me. Maybe I believed that once I made a commitment to something, I should go ahead and complete it. Maybe I looked at my getting married the same way I looked at other areas of my life which I did complete once I undertook them. For example, in education; I believe the Lord had allowed me to receive some great education in both the elementary and high school's I attended, as well as in college. In the area of sports, here too I had made some great accomplishments as a runner on my school's track teams. Whenever I finished a race, especially if our team had did well, I remember feeling great, particularly after all of the hard practicing we engaged in to prepare for those races. In the area of music, I felt a sense of accomplishment with my drum playing in rock bands I had been in. (As a side note, I wish I could say I felt a sense of accomplishment in the earning and handling of money, but no one in my family ever had any knowledge of that area.)

The point of all of this is that despite my upbringing in a seriously dysfunctional home with the life style that my mother had engaged in, when I got older, I was starting to come into my own world of minor accomplishments. Again, despite everything that had happened in my home life during my child-hood years, I thought to myself that I had turned out all right. Thus, I thought to myself why couldn't my married life be like that? That is to say, with everything that had gone "right" in my life in my young adult years, I may have been thinking, subconsciously anyway, that I could do this marriage thing with no problem. If I was able to accomplish those other areas of my life with little or no problem, I thought, then I should be able to do well in my married life also. The obvious difference here is that when it came to relationships, I lacked any healthy model in my own background. I only had that distorted view of how to interact with girls. Ultimately, I didn't know what true love for a woman looked like. I only knew what lust and infatuation looked like.

So what happened in my marriage later in life? To make a long story short, generally speaking, my wife came into the marriage with her own baggage of emotional stuff. Everything from our sex life to just our daily interactions with one another had suffered. We did have our moments of good times together, but I firmly believe each of us knew in our hearts that our marriage was a mistake. I think neither of us knew how to let true love fester or grow in us for each other. We tried the counseling circuit, both in the church and in the secular field. Nothing seemed to work. Eventually, I went back to seeking "love" in all the wrong places outside of my marriage. I would have affairs with women I met while at work. There were so many lies I would tell my wife of why I couldn't come home on certain nights, claiming that I was working late or working massive over-time in order to make more money. In reality, it was in these times that I was out with some other woman. All the while, I knew I was lost; I knew it was sin. I don't even use my upbringing as an excuse for what I did; it was just wrong.

Finally, my wife and I separated and then eventually, after some long litergation in the courts, got a divorce. It was a sad time for me. I felt anything but free. I blamed only myself for giving up on my marriage and not trying harder to make it work. In my heart, I forgave my wife for all of her own idiosyncrasies, but I carried around a guilt complex for some time. The only consolation was that we never had any children which obviously would have made things a lot worse. From the depths of my heart, I was sorry that my marriage was not a success like other families I had met in the church. I can only say that I continued to trek on, believing in the forgiving power of the shed blood of Jesus. That was all I could do.

Other Areas Realating To Sex & Relationships

There are obviously other areas relating to the general topic of sex and relationships of which I have not spoken about in this context of the sin-system of our world. I will attempt a brief mention of at least two other areas here.

(Homosexuality)

One area is the always controversial homosexual life style. In recent times, there has been a movement to have governments recognize homosexual unions as valid and legal marriages. One reason for this is to have employee benefits given to partners just as they are in hetero-sexual marriages. Indeed, many today believe that the homosexual life style is normal.

The scriptures, on the other hand, give a clear prohibition against homosexuality. (Leviticus 20:13 & Romans 1:26-27 are just two examples.) This, however, does not negate the love that God has for the homosexual person just as He has for any other sinner. At the same time, just as with any other sin, there needs to be a repentance on the part of the sinner in order to be in right relationship with God. In this work, I cannot and will not even scratch the surface in talking about all the various ramifications of the homosexual life style, such as the topic of how one becomes a homosexual in the first place, or what various studies have shown about that life style. Were those who subscribe to the homosexual life style all sexually abused by someone when they were young? The people that I have been acquainted with who are homosexuals were. Is that true for all homosexuals? I don't have the answer to that one. I can only go by what the scriptures say, and that is that the homosexual life style is not according to God's perfect plan for mankind. It is, however, a result of sin in some form or fashion.

(Pornography)

An area of our society which probably has the lowest form of the treatment of women is in the world of pornography. Here again, I can only make mention of some facts. In this industry, women are nothing more than objects of pleasure. Thus, they are reduced to the lowest common denominator in terms of their own character and their own self worth.

Over the years, we have seen the results of pornography for both those who engage in that industry, and those who watch it. Back in the 80's, a documentary on the PBS program "Frontline" entitled "Death of A Porn-Queen" gave a vivid description of the unfortunate life of mid-west girl named Colleen Applegate. The documentary, I thought, was well done, covering all the bases of the depravity of that industry. The subject of the documentary, Colleen, ended up getting addicted to drugs and eventually commiting suicide.

Mass murderer Ted Bundy, who was given capital punishment in Florida back in 1989, admitted before his execution in a taped interview with "Focus On The Family's" Dr. James Dobson that it was his addiction to pornography that led him to commit multiple murders against his female victims.

Ultimately, pornography isn't about love; it's about lust and the fulfillment of fleshly desires.

(Hollywood)

It should be obvious to everyone that Hollywood over the years has made major contributions to the culture of loose morals. Now a days, it's really nothing for any given movie to portray couples living together and having sex out of wedlock. It's only natural, one might say. Even in the area of violence, we see the glorification of killing all the time in many movies. "A hit", i.e. a murder, in a mob movie is all right because that's what everyone expects to happen. It may be what everyone expects, but in the real world it's sin.

What is the message that we're giving to our children and to the world by these movies? Is it ok to imitate these life styles of loose morality and violence?

(Different Cultures)

I want to end this chapter on sex, love, and marriage by briefly addressing how different cultures are contributing, sometimes perhaps unknowingly, to sin in our society.

I remember going to work one day and seeing a video that a fellow police officer had brought back from a trip he took to Italy. The video was of a TV game show that was on the air over there in Italy in which nude female dancers would come out to do their thing before and after each commercial break. Mind you, these dancers had nothing to do with the game actually being played by the contestants. In fact, at least according to the officer who brought in the video, nudity seemed to be pretty common in other European shows that he observed.

So one might ask the question, is it we over here in America who are too prudish, too uptight, too conservative when it comes to certain things like nudity? If we are this way, then my only reaction is thank God! But of course, even here in America we are not totally censored from nude displays on some cable channels. I hate to say it, but some of the programs that are shown on Latin television border on the obscene.

What is the point of all of this discussion? The point, in my opinion, is that these things are what are contributing to loose morals in our society. We know and see the results of these things everyday: unwed teenage mothers, mothers in poverty who for all practical purposes should hold off from getting pregnant and having multiple children year after year. Maybe this is why even Jesus said "The poor we will always have with us." (Matt. 26:11) Instead of abstaining from sex and pregnancy, at least until things would get better for them economically, some of the poor just continue to show no regard for their own families by doing whatever they please.

Am I saying that poor people should never have children, or that poor people should have more abortions? By no means is this what I'm saying. There does, however, I believe to be more of a need for education and for more discipline in the poor communities. In the 1960's, by the actions of one woman, Madeline O'Hara, all forms of prayer were eliminated from our nation's public schools. In the late 1980's and early 1990's, at least in the New York City public school system, condoms were distributed to any who wanted them. Now I ask you, what is the message that we sent to our youth with that move on behalf of our governing officials? Could it be, you're not allowed to pray in school, but it's ok to have sex at any age, just be careful? You be the judge.

(Conclusion)

In this chapter on sex, love and marriage, I have given some examples of how as a society, we are all messed up when it comes to relating to one another in truly loving ways. The topic of divorce is just one of those ways in which we have hurt one another. My personal testimony and brief history was to show some of my own idiosyncrasies in relating to the opposite sex. In the end, only God knows where as a society we will end up.

Do the cultures that have arranged marriages within their families have the answer to a more stable life style? Studies have shown that even those types of marriages have no guarantee of total happiness and are not immune from the trials of divorce.

We need to turn back to God and to His word to see how we should live. We need to do an in-depth study of Paul's 1st letter to the Corinthian Church, chapter 13, the chapter on what true love looks like. And even then, we need to fall on our hands and knees to seek God's guidance through the Holy Spirit on how we should be living.

VI

What Is The End Of It All?

A Review

In this book, I have attempted to spell out in plain, common language what are some of the ways that our world is in sin, that is, not living up to the standards that were originally intended for us to live in according to all that our creator desired for us. I call it the "sin-system of our world." My words were nothing in depth; I did not give any profound insights into any of the topics which I discussed. Rather, I just spoke generally about various areas of depravity that currently exist in our world. In point of fact, if we're all honest with ourselves, we already know these issues which I talked about to be true; that is, we already know that drug addiction and drug marketing are part of the sin system of our world; we already know that the love of money which leads to greediness and other crimes is sin; we know that various causes of poverty are sin; we know murder is sin, adultery is sin, ultimately, war can be considered sin. Why are all these things sin? Because they hurt people; they express the complete antithesis of love for one another. As the Apostle John writes in first epistle, "Whoever does not love does not know God, because God is love." (I John 4:8 NIV)

So the question might be asked that if we know all these things already, why write about them? I believe the answer to that is simply that we need to be reminded of our condition, that is to say that we need to be shown in a fresh new way what is the predicament that we are all in. We need to be shown again what is our destiny. Ultimately, we need to be shown again what was the purpose of Jesus' death on the cross. Is it just some ritual that we commemerate each Sunday at a church service? Or is it something more than that? Again, quoting from John's 1st epistle, "This is love: not that we loved God, but that He loved us and sent His Son as an atoning sacrifice for our sins." He goes on, "Dear friends, since God so loved us, we also ought to love one another." (I John 4:10 & 11)NIV

There's no other way of saying it; we are all lost without Christ. All of man's goodness could never measure up to God's righteousness (Isaiah 64:6) One more quote from John's epistle: "If we claim to be without sin, we deceive ourselves and the truth is not in us. If we confess our sins, He is faithful and just and will forgive us our sins and purify us from all unrighteousness." (I John 1:8&9) NIV

(My Personal Testimony)

What was the purpose of including my personal testimony in this writing? My purpose was simply to give an example of how we hurt one another, of how we take advantage of one another. The men who would come to my home just to have sex with my mother took advantage of her and used her for their own fleshly desires. As I had stated, my mother was probably abused herself as a young woman, maybe even abandoned by her own parents. Her lifestyle caused immeasurable hurt to me as a young boy because I knew in my heart that her way of living was wrong. Later in life, I would take advantage of women. The point of all of this, again, was to show how we hurt one another, ultimately, how we sin against one another.

Other Areas Not Covered

This book is not by any means all inclusive of every possible element of sin that exists in our world today. Indeed, there other topics which I have not addressed in this work. All one needs to do is to watch your nightly news on TV to see the multitude of other sins which I have not spoken about in this work. Permit me here, however, to talk to at least two other areas.

Islam & The Middle East Conflict

I have not spoken to the whole conflict in the Middle East and the current Islamic terrorist threat that exists throughout the world. I believe that the Muslim people have to make a decision for themselves. Either they are going to co-exist in a civilized world with other peoples who are not of their faith, or we will continue to have an atmosphere where every Muslim is suspect, and no true peace to be had anywhere that they abide.

There is a problem that exists, however. Unfortunately, the Quran, the bible of Islam, contains passages which say that the Muslim is to have nothing to do with the Christian and the Jew, or the "people of the book" as they call us, lest they become like us, another words becoming polluted with our ways.1 Other writings such as the "Hadith" contain extra messages, if you will, of the prophet Mohammed which some have used to enhance their view of the "need" for a holy war against the west. One passage specifically states that anyone who does not accept Mohammed as the prophet of Allah should be fought against.2

This is obviously a dilemma for any true Muslim in our current world. Many people outside of Islam don't even know scriptures like these exist. Of course, many who call themselves Christians are not even in tune with what the Bible says having never read it, much less having ever read the writings of any other religion. The point is, what does one do once he or she becomes fully aware of what their religion stands for? Does it make a change in their lives' for the better or for the worse? In the context of what we're speaking about here, what is the Muslim to do with passages like the ones described above?

It's possible that a Muslim might respond to this by saying that he's only fighting against everything that I myself have spoken about in this book, i.e. the sin-system of our world. What the Muslim is not aware of, however, is that there is a difference in how a true Christian would view the world system in contrast to how a Muslim extremist views it. For the Christian, there is indeed sin in our world. I've spoken to this already with various examples. However, the Christian can never physically or even mentally try to force anyone to accept their views of life. As a Christian, I don't have the right to throw you in jail, or worse execute you, if you don't accept Christ into your life. What I <u>can</u> do is to pray for you to some day not only accept Christ into your life, but that you will see the <u>need</u> to do so. I am also able to be responsible in the area of standing up for and lobbying for just causes and legislation that favors Biblical policies or ethics. But again, as a Christian, I am prohibited from engaging in any form of violence against non-believers.

The Word tells me that God deals with all evils according to His own plans and His own timing. "Vengeance is mine, and recompense, for the time when their foot shall slip; for the day of their calamity is at hand, and their doom comes swiftly. For the Lord will vindicate His people and have compassion on His servants..." (Deut. 32:35&36) RSV

So all this begs the question, is the one who sets off bombs against innocent people who happen to be not of the bomber's sect of religion in sin? I would say most definitely. In my mind, they are the newest members of the sin-system of our world. There's more I could say, but again, I believe it will be interesting to see with passing time how the Muslims deal with their own internal conflicts of living in a civilized world and what their own scriptures have to say about co-existing with non-believers. Personally, I believe as we draw closer to the end times, it will most likely get worse before it gets better. As the God of our fathers, Abraham, Issac, and Jacob, dealt justly with Babylon in the Old Testament, so will He once again deal with all the enemies of His children at the end of the age.

False Messiahs

Another area I have not spoken to is how from time to time, someone will come on the scene and proclaim to the world that he is the messiah. Back in the 70's during my aforementioned college years, a gentleman from South Korea named Rev. Moon came to America and claimed, subtlety at first, that he was the re-incarnation of Jesus the Messiah. Many were led astray by his followers who appeared to be genuine Christians.

Today, as I engage in writing this book, there is another man down in Texas, originally from Puerto Rico, who, like others before him, claims to be the messiah. The sad thing about this is that he is not without many followers.

The Bible tells us that in the last days there will be many false prophets and false messiahs. But we are not to be deceived for Jesus will return in the same way that He left, that is in the clouds, and every eye will see Him and finally recognize that indeed He is the Lord.

There's an interesting scripture in the Old Testament found in the book of Hosea, chapter 4, and verse 6. It reads "My people are destroyed for lack of knowledge; because you have rejected knowledge, I reject you from being a priest to me." The context of this passage is simply that God was rebuking His children Israel for forgetting about all of the laws that were given to them and for living like a harlot. In essence, Israel had once again rejected God and His ordinaces and was doing her own thing.

How has our world today done the same thing time and again just as the ancient Israelites did? In this book, I've only scratched the surface of the sins that I mentioned which shows our affinity with the ancient Israelites. In my last example above, the people who follow false prophets and false messiahs have made a major mistake. They have rejected the knowledge of the true and living God and of His Word. They may take scripture and turn it around for their own purposes, or take a passage out of context, thus not getting the full meaning of its message. In a sense, they are like the atheist who also has rejected the knowledge of God. Just as the spirit of the atheist is really a spirit of rebellion against any deity that they see as "controlling" them, so those who follow any whim that pleases their ears are also in rebellion against the truth.

We all have a choice, a free will, if you please. We can continue living as we so desire, that is, doing our own thing, rejecting the knowledge of God and of His word; continuing to look out for number 1, namely ourselves; not caring about whom we hurt just as long as we get what we want; or, we can truly seek the Lord, study His word, and truly love one another.

Paul says in II Timothy 2:15 "Study to show thyself approved unto God, a workman that needeth not to be ashamed, rightly dividing the word of truth." (KJV) The word "study" in this passage is used in the imperative sense, i.e. it's a command; it doesn't mean "if you want to" or "if you can". It means do it! The phrase "rightly dividing" in the ancient Greek simply means to dissect correctly. In essence, I'm told in this scripture that I have no excuse. My job is to get into the word, to study it, to dissect or take it apart, and then to apply it to myself. Anything short of this shows that I'm rejecting the true knowledge of God. Anything short of this also makes me vulnerable to lies and deceptions by those who would lead people astray.

How is this so, you might ask. If I don't know the word, if I don't spend time in it and study it, I could be susceptible to believing what anyone says or teaches without verifying it to be actually true. For example, I could say to you that the New Testament says to " hate your father and your mother" and to follow me. Now if we did nothing else and just took that phrase as it is, you have the potential for becoming part of a cult that would demand your total allegiance, demand all of your time, all of your money, and have you forget about everyone and everything else.

On the other hand, if we were to truly study the passage which contains that phrase mentioned above about hating your parents, and is found in the gospel of Luke, chapter 14 verse 26, we would see there that Jesus is giving various examples about the cost of being a disciple. The meaning of it all is that God should be number one in our lives; everything else is secondary. The word "hate" used in verse 26 in the ancient Greek simply means to "love less". It's not the vengeful kind of hate that we think of when we dislike something and might take a harmful action against. Our English language is unfortunately limited when it comes to the true expression or meaning of certain ideas. This is why it's important to engage in a deeper study of the word. Anything less only short-changes us and we can walk away not truly being fed.

Permit me one more general example. We've seen how the Apostle John proclaimed that "God is love." Can we imply from this statement that since God is love that there must not be anything in the after-life as a judgement for our actions and that neither is there any such thing as a place called hell? Well, this is exactly what some today would have everyone to believe. However, contrary to that form of thinking, the scripture is clear: "He that believeth on Him is not condemned; but he that believeth not is condemned already, because he hath not believed in the name of the only begotten Son of God." (John 3:18)KJV

So yes, God is love. He proved that on the cross. At the same time, and unfortunately you might say, some will be sent to that place where they will be separated from God for eternity. When Christ was crucified between two thieves, one mocked Christ, the other acknowledged Christ as the Lord. Jesus' response to that one, and that one only who recognized Jesus' Lordship was "Today you will be with me in paradise." (Luke 23:43)

The Return of Christ

The sin-system of our world, of which I have attempted to speak about in this book, will one day be ultimately done away with when Christ returns to earth. The question is when will that happen? There are different views all of which revolve around the concept of a tribulation period that will come on the earth unlike anything that was ever experienced before. There's a "pre-tribulation theory", a "mid-tribulation theory", and a "post-tribulation theory."

Simply speaking, the pre-trib theory, which is the one that most evangelical Christians hold to, states that the church, meaning all true believers who've committed their lives' to Christ, will be raptured out of the world before the start of this so-called tribulation period. The word "rapture", although not specifically found in the Bible, is spoken about in Paul's 1st letter to the Thessalonians, chapter 4, beginning at verse 15. It reads, "For this we declare to you by the word of the Lord, that we who are alive, who are left until the coming of the Lord, shall not precede those who have fallen asleep. For the Lord Himself will descend from heaven with a cry of command, with the archangel's call, and with the sound of the trumpet of God. And the dead in Christ will rise first; then we who are alive who are left, shall be caught up together with them in the clouds to meet the Lord in the air; and so we shall always be with the Lord. Therefore comfort one another with these words." (RSV)

Jesus Himself also mentions something of a rapture. In Matthew's gospel, chapter 24, the chapter that talks to what the tribulation period will look like, Jesus says, beginning at verse 38, "For as in the days before the flood, they were eating and drinking, marrying and giving in marriage, until the day when Noah entered the ark, and they did not know until the flood came and swept them all away, so will be the coming of the Son of man. Then two men will be in the field; one is taken and one is left. Two women will be grinding at the mill; one is taken and one is left. Watch therefore, for you do not know on what day your Lord is coming." (Matt. 24:38-42 RSV)

If this sounds like something out of "Star-Trek" to you, like "Beam me up, Scotty", don't worry, you're not alone. It *is* kind of weird. In our finite minds, we are unable to totally fathom what this whole rapture thing will look like. Yet, *it is* there in the Bible for all to read about.

As a review, the three theories are as follows: once again, for the pre-tribers, the church is raptured out of the world <u>before</u> the start of the tribulation period. The post-tribers believe the opposite, that is, they believe the church will not be exempt from going through the tribulation period and that the rapture will occur somewhere near the end of it all. The mid-tribers, on the other hand, believe that the church will only go through half of the tribulation period, and then one day, be taken out.

All of this coincides with another interesting event in scripture, namely the revelation of the "Anti-Christ". Just generally speaking, the Anti-Christ supposedly will be someone who will come on the scene and will be very charismatic. The world will be in chaos due to all kinds of wars going on, financial collapses, etc., etc. The Anti-Christ will be the one who somehow brings everyone together to have peace. After a certain period, perhaps 3 and a half years (½ of 7 years, the believed period of the tribulation found in the book of Daniel), the person of the Anti-Christ will set himself up as the messiah or God and will demand total allegiance only to him. Is this when the true church is raptured as the mid-tribers believe?

The Point Of It All

The bottom line to all of this is that no matter which theory you subscribe to, Jesus is coming back for a church without spot or blemish. How was this spot or blemish removed? It was removed on Calvary's cross.

We don't know when Christ will return. The Bible says He will return like a thief in the night. Those who would predict the exact date of His return are only fooling themselves.

If you were around in the 1970's, you might recall both a book and even a movie by the author Hal Linsey entitled "The Late Great Planet Earth." I recall seeing that movie, which by the way played in regular movie theathers for a short time, and thinking to myself that the world was going to end any day now. Other authors had jumped on the band wagon at that time. The Rev. Dave Wilkerson with his short film "The Road To Armageddon" was another example of something that made us think that the final curtain was about to be drawn. Well, as I am writing this book in the year 2008, the world obviously hasn't ended yet. That's not to say that it can't end at any time, because it will. The question that should really be asked is a two-fold question, I believe: 1st, how are you occupying, or spending your time here on earth before either Christ returns or it comes time for you to die? 2nd, are you in right relationship with Christ in the first place? Do you think that you're really good enough to stand before the throne of God and get into heaven on your own merits? After all, you may say you go to church every Sunday, you pray three times a day, you give money to the poor. These are all good. But as Christ said to the young rich ruler, "go sell what you possess and give to the poor....and come follow me." (Matt. 19:21) That ruler walked away dejected because he had much, another words, he wasn't ready to give it all up to follow Christ, i.e. to make Christ number one in his life.

In my mind, there's still a lot of stuff that the world will go through before Christ returns. I believe there will come a time that the general culture will look down on all religions as the cause of our world problems. There may even come a time that religions will be banned, just as in the days of the height of Communism where religious groups were forced to meet secretly. I don't know for sure. It might be a time as is sung about in the tune "Imagine" by John Lennon where the lyric goes: "Imagine there's nothing to kill or die for,....and <u>no religion too</u>." I could see our world headed in that direction. To me, <u>that</u> would be the perfect time for a tribulation period to start. But again, that's just my opinion; don't take that as gospel.

As already stated, Christ will return someday. We don't understand it all. We can't comprehend how it will be. Our minds are limited. In fact, outside of what we have in scripture, we can't even comprehend God Himself. I mean think of it; an infinite being with no beginning and no end! Who can understand that alone? To us here on earth, everything has a beginning and an end. Likewise in other areas, for example, scripture encourages us to pray for one another. Well, how come when I pray for a sick person, that person may receive a healing, and at other times someone else whom I pray for doesn't get healed? Truly, I don't have an answer. All I do know is that I'm told to pray. As I see it, my job is only to obey and do.

We can only go by what the Word tells us and accept it by faith. "Beloved, we are God's children now; it does not yet appear what we shall be, but we know that when He appears, we shall be like Him, for we shall see Him as He is. And everyone who thus hopes in Him purifies himself as He is pure." (I John 3:2&3) RSV

Some Final Thoughts

Throughout my career as a New York City Police Officer, I had the opportunity to be assigned to some exciting events. For example, I remember being assigned to cover the Nelson Mandella visit to New York. After his release from a South African prison, everyone treated him almost as if <u>he</u> were God. His visit to NY was a grand event, especially for the Black community.

The Sin System Of Our World

1995 : Opening day in April of the baseball season at Yankee Stadium. Even though it wasn't my official post on that day, I managed to get inside anyway.

The Sin System Of Our World

2000 : At the Yankee victory parade in October in lower Manhattan after beating the NY Mets in the Subway World Series. With me is fellow Police Officer Steve Baranski. It was a joyous time for all New Yorkers while the rest of the country probably didn't care. (The following year, all joy would be gone after Sept. 11th.)

Other exciting events in my tenure as a cop included victory parades for NY sports teams whenever they won a championship. One assignment I'll never forget is being assigned inside Yankee Stadium for game 2 of the Subway World Series between the Yankees and the Mets in October of 2000. I watched the whole game and got paid time and half overtime for it!

The point of these examples given above is that these were afairs where men were giving glory to men. It's natural to cheer on a great sports figure, or to give praise to some political figure who stands up for a great and just cause. But I often wondered to myself, how will it be when Christ returns to earth? Will there be the same or even greater exuberance from crowds of people as there have been in the past for worldly figures? Will the same people who cheer for their favorite movie stars as they walk down the red carpet at the Oscars be there to cheer on Christ as He makes His glorious re-entry onto the earth's scene? For me, <u>that</u> will be the ultimate detail to be assigned to, not as a cop, but as a believer who awaited the return of the one who died for me!

I like to close this work of mine with a quote from a book I read when I was a young Christian in college back in the 70's. I hope it will speak to you. The book is entitled "Knowing God" by J.I. Packer: "If we know ourselves at all, we know we are not fit to face Him. What then are we to do? The New Testament answer is: call on the coming judge to be your present savior. As judge, He is the law, but as savior He is the gospel. Run from Him now, and you will meet Him as judge then - and without hope. Seek Him now, and you will find Him...."[3]

Notes

1. The Quran; Surat Al-Maida, 5 Section 8: vs. 51

2. An - Nawawi, Forty Hadith (Cambridge, U.K.: Islamic Text Society, 1997), Hadith #8, pg. 46

3. J.I. Packer, Knowing God (Downers Grove, Illinois: Inter-Varsity Press, 1973), pg. 133

Bibliography

An-Nawawi's <u>Forty Hadith.</u> Cambridge, U.K.: Islamic Text Society, 1997.

Franzmann, Martin & Roehrs, Walter <u>Concordia Self-Study Commentary.</u> St. Louis, Mo: Concordia Publishing House, 1979.

<u>Holy Bible</u>. KJV = King James Version
NIV = New International Version
RSV = Revised Standard Version

Lindsey, Hal <u>The Late Great Planet Earth.</u> Grand Rapids, Mi: Zondervan, 1970.

Packer, J.I. <u>Knowing God.</u> Downers Grove, Illinois: Inter-Varsity Press, 1973.

<u>Quran.</u>

Stott, John <u>Basic Christianity</u>, Downers Grove, Illinois: Inter-Varsity Press, 1974.

Walther, C.F.W. <u>The Proper Distinction Between Law & Gospel.</u> St. Louis, Mo.: Concordia Publishing House.

Epilogue

A Closing Prayer

If you believe anything I've written in this book is true, then I encourage you to recite this prayer of repentance. You can use my words or use your own; it doesn't matter, just as long as you give it from your heart.

"Almighty God and Father, I come to you now in prayer to say I'm sorry for all that I've done which was contrary to your will for me. I'm sorry for taking any path in life which wasn't the path that you wanted me to go down. I'm sorry for hurting anyone that I did whether emotionally or even physically. I ask for your forgiveness through the shed blood of your Son Jesus Christ. Please cleanse my soul and my spirit and come into my life. I commit the rest of my days into your hands and ask that you would lead me where you would have me to go and show me what you would have me to do. I thank you that you sent your son to die for my sins. Guide me and teach me now in all of your ways; I ask this in the name of your Son Jesus Christ who lives and reigns with you in the unity of the Holy Spirit, one God forever and ever, Amen."

If you sincerely prayed this prayer from your heart, then I encourage you to next find a church where the true Gospel is preached, and where there is good fellowship and Bible study, not just on Sundays, but on various days throughout the week. We can't walk this walk alone. We need those spiritual vitamins just mentioned: prayer (I Thess. 5:17), fellowship (Heb. 10:25), and

Bible study (II Tim. 3:16). This also includes our worship time and our financial giving to His kingdom work.

God bless you on your new journey.

My Personal Prayer of Thanksgiving

This final prayer is my personal prayer of thanksgiving to the Lord which I felt inspired to include at the end of this book. It's just my way of saying thanks for all that the Lord has allowed me to experience. As you read it, you may not be familiar with the places I mention, particularly if you've never visited New York, but hopefully you can get a sense of what I'm trying to say here, and maybe it will inspire you to write your own prayer of thanksgiving for the places and things the Lord has allowed <u>you</u> to experience.

"Almighty God, I just want to say thanks for all the things you've allowed me to experience. I thank you first of all for allowing me to be born in the greatest city in the world, New York City. When I think of all the places and things NY has to offer, I see that I was truly blessed being here. I think of the parks I used to play in as a child, like Riverside Park, and then later in life Central Park; I thank you for those specific places and what fun I used to have playing there with my best friends Angelo and Michael. I thank you for other fun places like the beach at Coney Island and all of the amusement rides that I enjoyed there. I hope it never closes so that others can experience the same fun that I had.

I thank you for other cultural places in NY like the Museum of Natural History; for Broadway theaters where I saw various plays later in life; for 'Shakespear In The Park' which were great <u>free</u> plays that I got to see. I thank you for the world of music, specifically rock-n-roll, and how my friends and I were able to see almost all of the top groups of my day at various venues like the Brooklyn Fox, Madison Square Garden, and the Fillmore East.

I thank you for how you gave me a talent to play the drums so that I could imitate all of my favorite groups along with other musicians (Willie, Alberto, Frank, Johnny, Bello & Dave). Then later in life, I thank you for allowing me to play for you in church with various members of our worship teams.

I thank you Lord for all of the education I received from grammar school (Holy Name of Jesus), to high school (Rice High School), to college (Hunter College & John Jay College). I thank you for all the friends I made in those days of my school years, and even though it's been a long time since I've seen any of them, I pray that they all would come to have a personal relationship with you if they haven't done so already in their lives', so that we can see each other again in heaven.

I thank you for the memory of my cousins whom I also haven't seen since I was a kid. I frankly don't even know if they remember me; but it doesn't matter, the point is I remember them, and just as with my friends, I pray I will see my cousins again in heaven only because they too came to a personal knowledge of Jesus and of His death on the cross for us.

I thank you for my parents. Eventhough they weren't the perfect parents, still they did provide for me the basic needs. I thank you Lord for how you protected me and brought me through the hard times when my mother was living her life of prostitution. I hold no animosity towards my mother nor towards my father. I can only hope that they are with you in heaven.

I thank you Lord for how you used other believers in my college days to reveal yourself to me in a personal way.

I thank you for how you protected me during my time on the police force. Truly there were some fun times and some hairy moments during my time on the job. But you were there with me through it all. And even when I back-slid, you allowed me to see the stupidity of my actions and brought me back with your grace.

Finally, I thank you for my wife Liz, for how she has shown me what true love looks like by all the things she has done for me.

Thank you Lord, in Jesus' name I pray all these things, Amen."

About The Author

Ed Steele is a retired New York City Police Officer and native of that same town. He is not a theologian nor an ordained minister of any particular denomination. He is simply a guy who wants to share how he sees the gospel message of Jesus Christ. Ed continues to live and work in his beloved NY Metro area. This is his 1st attempt at publishing a literary work. More importantly, he loves and serves the Lord. You might be able to relate to some of the things Ed talks about in his book, and then again, you might not. His only desire is that you would be open to reading what he has to say. Any comments or questions about his book can be directed to Ed's e-mail at: **steeleman2@verizon.net**

www.ingramcontent.com/pod-product-compliance
Lightning Source LLC
LaVergne TN
LVHW041541070526
838199LV00046B/1782